Date: 6/29/15

J 975.918 SIP
Sipperley, Keli.
The old fort at St. Augustine

D1209532

PALM BEACH COUNTY
LIBRARY SYSTEM
3650 SUMMIT BLVD.
WEST PALM BEACH, FL 33406

THE OLD FORT AT ST. AUGUSTINE

Keli Sipperley

Rourke
Educational Media

rourkeeducationalmedia.com

Scan for Related Titles
and Teacher Resources

Before Reading:

Building Academic Vocabulary and Background Knowledge

Before reading a book, it is important to tap into what your child or students already know about the topic. This will help them develop their vocabulary, increase their reading comprehension, and make connections across the curriculum.

1. *Look at the cover of the book. What will this book be about?*
2. *What do you already know about the topic?*
3. *Let's study the Table of Contents. What will you learn about in the book's chapters?*
4. *What would you like to learn about this topic? Do you think you might learn about it from this book? Why or why not?*
5. *Use a reading journal to write about your knowledge of this topic. Record what you already know about the topic and what you hope to learn about the topic.*
6. *Read the book.*
7. *In your reading journal, record what you learned about the topic and your response to the book.*
8. *After reading the book complete the activities below.*

Content Area Vocabulary
Read the list. What do these words mean?

ammunition
artillery
bastions
coquina
forged
masonry
medieval
mortar
siege
treaty

After Reading:

Comprehension and Extension Activity

After reading the book, work on the following questions with your child or students in order to check their level of reading comprehension and content mastery.

1. *Explain the history the Native Americans had with the fort at St. Augustine.* (Summarize)
2. *How do the coquina stone make the walls stronger?* (Asking questions)
3. *Explain how the fort changed throughout the years depending on who controlled it.* (Summarize)
4. *Why were France and Britain interested in St. Augustine and the surrounding territory?* (Inferring)
5. *Have you visited a historical landmark before? Why do you think people want to preserve historical places?* (Text to self connection)

Extension Activity

Show causes and effects! Using the book, choose at least four different events that effected the fort at St. Augustine. Looking at those events write down the cause(s) and describe the effect(s). Create a visual representation such as an illustrated timeline, to present to your classmates or parents to teach them about the importance and history of the fort in St. Augustine, Florida.

TABLE OF CONTENTS

Attack in the Night 4

Shells Secure St. Augustine 7

Small but Mighty 9

Enduring Strength 14

An American Uprising 16

Protection Becomes a Prison 18

A Symbol of Struggle and Strength 22

Visiting the Old Fort 26

Timeline 29

Glossary 30

Index 31

Show What You Know 31

Websites to Visit 31

About the Author 32

Chapter 1

ATTACK IN THE NIGHT

English pirates rowed silently toward the shore of St. Augustine in 1668, their approach cloaked by the darkness of the night. With little warning, Robert Searle and his men laid **siege** to the town, taking what they could and burning the rest as residents took cover in the woods and soldiers tried to fend them off from the cover of rotting, wooden forts.

St. Augustine is the nation's oldest permanently occupied European settlement. It was founded 55 years before the Plymouth Colony.

The attack left many dead, and the residents without food, supplies and **ammunition**. It also inspired the queen regent of Spain to provide funding for a new fort to protect the important Spanish town.

Freedom Fact!

An English sailor who joined Drake on the English expedition against Spain described St. Augustine as a "city built all of timber … or bodies of trees set upright and close together."

Sir Francis Drake

Robert Searle's attack was not the first devastating blow to the Spanish shipping hub. About 100 years before, Francis Drake was appointed by Queen Elizabeth of England to lead an expedition to attack Spanish settlements in the Americas. Under orders from the queen, Drake and his crew of 2,000 men attacked and set fire to St. Augustine in 1586.

In historical documents you will often see the word circa before a date when the exact date is not known. Circa means approximately or about.

Sir Francis Drake circa (1540–1596)

St. Augustine was an important territory for Spain to protect, especially as colonists from England and France began to settle nearby. But the forts built by the Spanish settlers were not strong enough to withstand harsh attacks.

The damp Florida weather warped and weakened the wood used to construct them. They needed something stronger. Would you believe they chose to use tiny shells?

St. Augustine, Florida was established in 1565. It was created to protect the trade sea routes from the English and the French expansions.

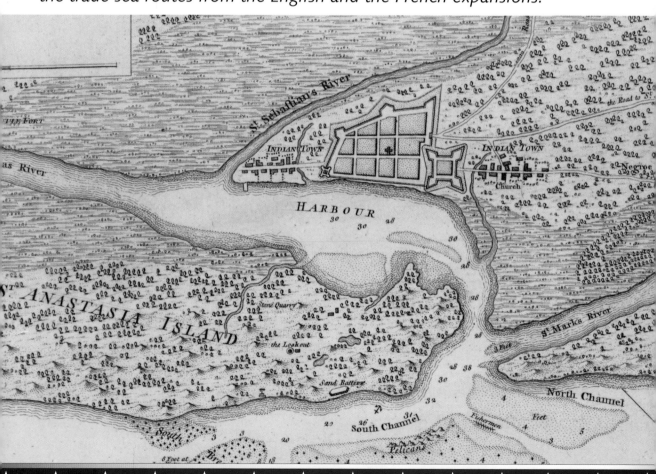

Chapter 2

SHELLS SECURE ST. AUGUSTINE

In 1672 military engineers and stonemasons from Spain traveled to St. Augustine to begin construction on the fort. This time, there would be no wood. Instead they used **coquina**, which means tiny shell in Spanish.

Oyster shells were baked until they became a fine white powder called lime. The lime was allowed to age, sometimes for a full year, before it was mixed with sand and water to make **mortar**.

Freedom Fact!

Coquina is made from the shells of small clams that fused together over thousands of years. The shell stone for the fort was quarried from Anastasia Island, a barrier island off the coast of St. Augustine. It is only found in a handful of places around the world.

During the next 23 years, the fort grew tall and wide. More than 400,000 stone blocks were made by hand and set in place by Spanish workers and Native Americans. They were not sure how strong a fort made of shells would be, so they built the walls facing the ocean 19 feet (5.8 meters) thick.

In 1695 the fort, Castillo de San Marcos, was complete. And the future of St. Augustine, and the United States, would soon be set in stone.

Freedom Fact!

The Castillo de San Marcos is a **masonry** star fort and the largest of its kind in the United States. It has four full **bastions**: the San Pedro, the San Agustin, the San Carlos, and the San Pablo.

San Pedro

San Pablo

San Agustin

San Carlos

Chapter 3

SMALL BUT MIGHTY

Seven years after the last stone was laid at Castillo de San Marcos, British soldiers led by Governor James Moore of nearby South Carolina attacked St. Augustine in 1702. More than 1,200 residents fled to the fort, which sheltered them as the long battle waged.

Governor James Moore
(1650–1706)

Moore and his troops tried to bombard the fort with cannon fire, but the cannon balls bounced off the coquina walls. Instead of crumbling, the tiny shells absorbed the blasts!

The British were not easily defeated. The attacks wore on for nearly two months before Moore and his men retreated, setting fire to everything in the town as they left. But the fort held strong and kept the residents safe.

Freedom Fact!

The fort included a central plaza, drinking water wells, a chapel and a furnace to heat cannon balls before firing them at wooden ships.

A reenactment of the Spanish in control of the fort.

The damage caused by the cannon balls can still be seen on the walls of the fort to this day.

Mystery Revealed

The tiny air spaces between the shells in coquina stone are the secret to its strength. When a cannon ball hits a wall of coquina, the impact presses the shell pieces inward against the air spaces. The air absorbs most of the force from the **artillery** fire. The wall may be dented, but it won't crack or crumble from the impact.

Chapter 4

ENDURING STRENGTH

When war between England and Spain began again in 1739, it wasn't long before the strength of Castillo de San Marcos was tested again. British General James Oglethorpe brought an army from Georgia to attack St. Augustine. The British set up forces on Anastasia Island, where the Spanish mined the coquina for Castillo de San Marcos.

The fort was blasted by the British for 27 days, but the strength of its walls held fast, and so did the city.

*General James Oglethorpe
(1696–1785)*

For 300 years, the shell walls of Castillo de San Marcos have remained impenetrable to enemy weapons, surviving conflicts between nations, settlers, Native Americans and the pirates who roamed the Atlantic coast.

When Britain did manage to take possession of St. Augustine in 1763, its fort and the rest of Florida from Spain, it was not by force.

The **Treaty** of Paris, which ended the Seven Years War, gave Britain the Florida territory. The land was split into East and West Florida. The British made St. Augustine the capital of East Florida and renamed its mighty fortress Fort St. Marks.

Last page of the Treaty of Paris, 1783

Chapter 5

AN AMERICAN UPRISING

In addition to Florida, the Treaty of Paris gave Great Britain control of French territories in America, expanding its power in the New World. But with the threat from France eliminated, residents of Britain's thirteen colonies were ready to free themselves from British rule.

This 1763 map shows how North America was divided at that time.

By 1775 the American Revolutionary War began. In 1776 Thomas Jefferson drafted the Declaration of Independence, proclaiming the colonies as a newly formed nation: The United States of America. But East Florida remained faithful to the British Empire. The fort at St. Augustine, once a shelter from British invasion, became a prison for Britain's captives, including two men who signed the Declaration of Independence.

*Thomas Jefferson
(1743–1826)*

The end of the war won freedom from European rule for the colonies in 1783, and Florida was returned to Spain. It was not until 1822 that East and West Florida joined the United States as a single U.S. territory. But the fort, renamed Fort Marion in 1825, to honor Revolutionary War hero Francis Marion, had not seen its last prisoner.

Rebels

Arthur Middleton and Edward Rutledge, signers of the Declaration of Independence, were among the rebels held prisoner at the fort. They were released at the end of the war in 1783.

*Arthur Middleton
(1742–1787)*

*Edward Rutledge
(1749–1800)*

Chapter 6

PROTECTION BECOMES A PRISON

As the young nation grew, American settlers were eager to acquire more land to grow cotton and other crops. But territories belonging to Native Americans stood in the way. To make room for progress, President Andrew Jackson decided to remove them from their homelands and relocate the Native Americans to unsettled lands west of the Mississippi River.

Andrew Jackson (1767–1845)

The Indian Removal Act was signed into law by President Jackson on May 28, 1830.

Though some tribes agreed to negotiate with the new American government, many Native Americans resisted. A treaty was signed with some Seminole tribe leaders in Florida in 1932, but other Seminoles fled into the Florida Everglades.

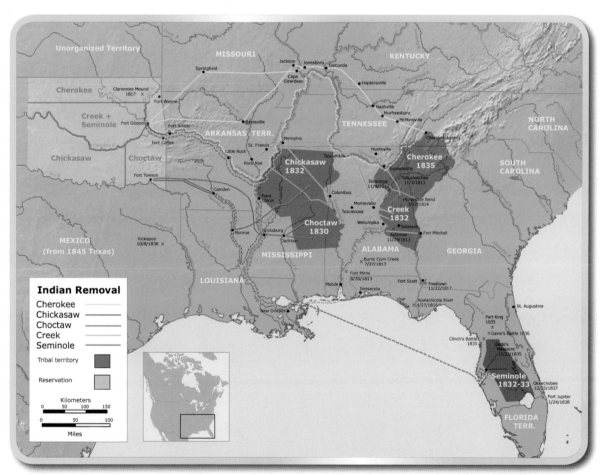

This map depicts the routes of what was known as the Trail of Tears, when the Indian Removal Act forced Native Americans out of the Southeastern U.S.

When U.S. troops arrived to enforce the treaty, which required the tribe to relocate, the Seminoles were ready for war. Their leader, Chief Osceola, was the government's fiercest enemy in the resistance.

After years of fighting, Osceola presented a flag of truce in hopes of negotiating with the U.S. forces. But the Seminole warrior was captured instead and imprisoned at the fort in St. Augustine in 1837. He died shortly afterward.

Chief Osceola (1804–1838)

The fort was used again in the decades to come as a prison for many other Native Americans as the fight over territory in the New World waged on.

Flags Over St. Augustine

Many flags have flown over the fort.

The First Spanish Period 1565 - 1763

The British Period 1763 - 1784

The Second Spanish Period 1784 - 1821

The First American Period 1821 - 1861

The Confederate Period 1861-1862

The Second American Period 1862 – 1900

Chapter 7

A SYMBOL OF STRUGGLE AND STRENGTH

After falling into disrepair, the fort underwent a makeover from U.S. Army engineers in 1842. It was last used as a defensive fort during the American Civil War from 1861 to 1865. Remarkably, in the centuries it was used, the fort never fell to an enemy! Control of the fort only changed hands through military agreements or treaties.

The drawbridge at Castillo de San Marcos.

After serving more than 200 years, the fort was removed from the United States' list of active military bases and declared a national monument. In 1942, the fort's original name, Castillo de San Marcos, was restored.

While not always filled with water, this is a moat around Castillo de San Marcos.

Freedom Fact!

*The fort's design is based on the bastion system developed by Italy in the 1600s. Much like **medieval** castles, the bastion design lowers the walls and relies on mounds of earth around the outside to further strengthen them. At each corner of the fort, the Spanish added circular towers to provide protection from every angle. A moat was built and drawbridges were added to secure access to the interior of the structure.*

moat

drawbridge

tower

Today, the Castillo de San Marcos still stands stark and gray over the St. Augustine harbor. Its mighty walls strong against the enemies of time and harsh weather, a reminder of America's past, St. Augustine's Spanish heritage and centuries of battles waged for land and power in the New World.

The fort, which served alternately as both a shelter and a prison, also symbolizes the struggles of settlers and Native Americans as a new, united nation was **forged**.

Chapter 8

VISITING THE OLD FORT

You can visit the Castillo de San Marcos every day of the year except December 25th. The fort opens daily at 8:45 a.m. and the ticket booth closes at 5:00 p.m.

Artifacts from the 18th and 19th centuries still adorn the fort today as reminders of the past.

About 3,500 people visit the fort every day in the summertime and during holidays! If you decide to visit during the peak visitor times, plan some extra time for your visit since it can get quite crowded.

Inside the fort, you can check out exhibits, look out at the view from the top, and see weapons demonstrations by actors dressed in period costumes reflecting the fort's storied history.

A film is shown every hour that highlights weapons used to defend the fort and other details from its past as a mighty fortress protecting Florida's shores from pirates and other invaders.

Reenactments show what colonial soldiers might have looked like as they fired cannons from the fort.

During your visit, be sure to get an up close look at the walls, where you will be able to see the tiny shells that make up the stones that saved St. Augustine.

TIMELINE

1565 —— *Pedro Menéndez de Avilés founds St. Augustine.*

1586 —— *St. Augustine is attacked and burned by British forces led by Francis Drake.*

1668 —— *English pirates led by Robert Searle, also known as John Davies, attack and burn St. Augustine.*

1672 —— *The Spanish begin construction of a new fort, Castillo de San Marcos, to protect St. Augustine from pirates, nearby English settlers and to shore up Spanish America's defenses in the New World.*

1695 —— *The construction of Castillo de San Marcos is completed.*

1702 —— *British forces attack St. Augustine and the fort, but retreat two months later when their firepower cannot penetrate the fort.*

1739 —— *The British attack St. Augustine and the fort again. Again, they are unsuccessful.*

1776-1783 *The American Revolution eventually frees the colonies from British rule and returns Florida to Spain.*

1825 —— *Castillo de San Marcos is renamed Fort Marion by the United States for Revolutionary War hero Francis Marion.*

1836 —— *Seminole tribe leader Chief Osceola is captured by U.S. forces and imprisoned in the fort.*

1861 —— *The Civil War begins. Florida secedes from the United States.*

1865 —— *The Civil War ends.*

1924 —— *Fort Marion is declared a National Monument.*

1942 —— *Fort Marion is returned to its original name, Castillo de San Marcos.*

GLOSSARY

ammunition (am-yuh-NISH-uhn): objects such as bullets or shells fired from weapons

artillery (ahr-TIL-ur-ee): large firearms such as cannons or rockets

bastions (BAS-chenz): some place or something that gives protection against attack

coquina (ko-KE-nuh): a soft whitish limestone formed of broken shells and corals cemented together and used for building

forged (forjd): to move forward steadily but gradually

masonry (MAY-suhn-ree): something built of stone, brick, or concrete

medieval (mee-DEE-vuhl): of or having to do with the Middle Ages

mortar (MOR-tur): a mixture of lime, sand, water, and cement that is used to hold bricks and stones together

siege (seej): the surrounding of a place such as a castle or city to cut off supplies and then wait for those inside to surrender

treaty (TREE-tee): a formal written agreement between two or more countries

INDEX

Britain 15, 16

British 9, 11, 14, 15, 16

coquina 7, 10, 14

Drake, Francis 5

England 5, 6, 14

Florida 6, 15, 16, 17, 19, 27

France 6, 16

Marion, Francis 17

Moore, James 9

Native Americans 8, 15, 19, 20, 25

New World 16, 20, 24

Oglethorpe, James 14

Osceola 20

pirates 4, 15, 27

Searle, Robert 4, 5

Seminole 19, 20

Spain 5, 6, 7, 14, 15, 17

Spanish 5, 6, 7, 8, 14, 24

The Indian Removal Act 19

Treaty of Paris 15, 16

SHOW WHAT YOU KNOW

1. Why was it important for Spain to protect the city of St. Augustine?
2. What made the Castillo de San Marcos so strong that cannon balls could not damage it?
3. What does the fort symbolize about America's history?
4. Which powers have controlled the fort since it was built?
5. How was control of the fort exchanged between nations?

WEBSITES TO VISIT

www.teachingflorida.org/article/the-castillo-de-san-marcos

www.nationalparks.org/explore-parks/castillo-de-san-marcos-national-monument

www.nps.gov/casa/index.htm

ABOUT THE AUTHOR

Keli Sipperley is a multimedia journalist and children's book author in Tampa, Florida. She enjoys writing stories about interesting moments, fun places, and people who help others in their communities. She has two sons and two daughters who love reading and writing as much as she does.

Meet The Author!
www.meetREMauthors.com

© 2015 Rourke Educational Media

All rights reserved. No part of this book may be reproduced or utilized in any form or by any means, electronic or mechanical including photocopying, recording, or by any information storage and retrieval system without permission in writing from the publisher.

www.rourkeeducationalmedia.com

PHOTO CREDITS: Cover Page © benkrut; Title Page © Bertl123; Page 4 © Shippee; Page 5 © Devon Buckland Abbey; Page 6, 8 , 14, 17, 18, 20, 22 © Library of Congress; Page 9 © Jacque Reich/Wikipedia; Page 10 Jacque Reich/Wikipedia Daniel Schwen/Wikipedia; Page 12 © Sakala, Page 13 © Anna Abramskaya; Page 15 © National Archives, Page 16 © Emanuel Bowen/PublishedLondon; Page 17 © Jacque Reich/Wikipedia, Benjamin West; Page 19 © Nikater; Page 21 © Ningyou, Hoshie/Ignaciogavira/Hansen BCN/SanchoPanza, jacobolous, Ariane Schmid; Page 23 © William Henry Jackson, nps; Page 24, 25 © Don Fink; Page 26 © gacooksy; page 27 © Paulbr; Page 28 © William Silver

Edited by: Luana Mitten

Cover design by: Renee Brady
Interior design by: Renee Brady

Library of Congress PCN Data

The Old Fort at St. Augustine / Keli Sipperley
(Symbols of Freedom)
 ISBN 978-1-63430-041-4 (hard cover)
 ISBN 978-1-63430-071-1 (soft cover)
 ISBN 978-1-63430-100-8 (e-Book)
Library of Congress Control Number: 2014953356

Printed in the United States of America, North Mankato, Minnesota

Also Available as: